GW01086008

C A

C A P E R S

Design

JAMES SPERRY

Illustrations

ROBYN THORN

Published by - J & S PUBLISHING PLYMOUTH.

Printed in Great Britain July 1997.

ISBN 0 9523395 1 X

From the pen of **ROBYN THORN**

Especially for CHRISTINE

With warm wishes from Robyn Thorn.

Special thanks to all our friends
for their help with the research on Cats

STRAY

I had you from a kitten, a tiny stray
Found your body lifeless, as you lay
A kiss of life was so gently breathed
Working together, cheating death indeed.

Your weak little body took nourishment
I then had a pet who was heaven sent
Now you are mine, and I am yours
My devoted companion, on all fours.

WELCOMING

It's nice to come home
And not feel so alone
To a welcoming stare
With you cat in my chair

ROSES

Whispering breezes, nodding flowers
Seems to keep you amused for hours
But don't go near my lovely roses
They have claws that scratch noses.

NOTICEABLE

Nobody's noticed but me
No one else can see
When your eyes blink
You always seem to wink.

CONTENTED

Smooth and glossy silky fur
Whilst I stroke, you always purr
So warm and contented, on my lap
Comfy too, as you take a quiet nap
If the doorbell rings, or the phone
You don't appreciate being alone
Following me about, like a shadow
Backwards and forwards, to and fro.

BONNET

My neighbour returned one day
In his car from a distance away
Stationary, heat rose from it
You immediately leapt on the bonnet.

PURR

My neighbours car is so small
But he doesn't mind at all
Whilst other engines roar
His just purrs, you even more.

The engine is so smooth
You hardly hear it move
And the paint work gleams
Until Paw prints cover the sheen's.

MOTH

It's nice to sit down, have a good read
This book's so good, just what I need
What's that fluttering, oh, only a moth
Get down cat, you're sure to fall off.

This story is quite gripping
Mystery deepens, so much plotting
Stop reaching up under the lamp
You'll fall and knock my lovely plant.

Cont.

Now I've lost my page, get down
Little wonder, I always frown
Will you behave, stop leaping up
I know it's a big one. WILL YOU STOP.

Oh no, your on the standard lampshade
You'll lose your balance, need my aid
The moth's now flown to another light
And now you're burnt, a sorry sight.

AIRING

You know you're in the wrong place
So don't scowl and pull a face
The airing cupboard is for clothes
Not for you to have a doze.

ANGRY

Your tail flicks, when your angry
I think you would almost agree
And when I try to calm you down
All I get is a furrowed frown
So why are you moody, and upset
Perhaps It's the visit to the vet.

WASH TIME

You wash yourself so thoroughly
It does take ages, so I let you be
Your tongue is rough. it does the trick
Just how many times, do you have to lick.

HOBBY

When I think you're patiently sitting
I can then, get on with my knitting
But suddenly, my wool will zoom
Speeding right around the room
And you getting in such a tangle
Between furniture, at every angle
My stitches drop, two, three, four
As you dash and whiz around the floor.

NOD AND WINK

Whiskers and paws
A tail and claws
Vibrating purr
A silken fur
Bristling mood
A lot of food
A tongue so pink
Eye's that wink
A soft damp nose
Teeth that close.

DIZZY

The postman's bike fell
Crashed to the floor. Hell
The wheel made a whirring sound
You jumped on a merry-go-round.

AROMA'S

Empty jars that are saved
For pickles, jam, when made
Stored in a spare room
Where your apt to loom.

And to your delight
Jars not shut tight
Have a lingering smell
Purrfect when you inhale.

PROVING

Baking my own loaves
I had to warm the stove
And once I made some dough
It had to be proved, like so.

In the warmth rising just fine
And the smell was so divine
But When I removed the tray
Amongst the bread you did lay.

FLOUR

CAT FLAP

I've had a cat flap conveniently fitted
To save being disturbed, when you flitted
Opening the doors, got quite draughty
At long last, I got ever so crafty.

BREAKFAST

When I get the milk each morning
The cat appears, without warning
Yes. The cream at the top is yours
Patiently waiting as It slowly pours
Whiskers covered, nose is too
There is no more, go away shoo
Hopefully now for my breakfast
In peace and quiet, at long last.

POOH

A new brand of food for you
You are unsure, and sniff, Pooh
Then you empty it on the ground
Why must you pussy-foot around
Now it's in the dustbin
All I can do is just grin.

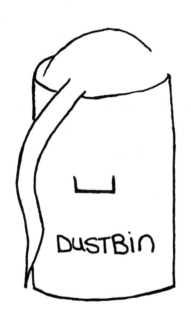

LUNCH

Whilst I was cooking a chicken
You wouldn't leave the kitchen
Rubbing my legs, also my toes
Until you got the parson's nose.

You still weren't satisfied
My own lunch, I had to hide
I was hungry, so shooed you outside
From the window ledge, you spied.

DESERT

Why do you always look so hurt
Just as I'm eating a nice desert
I know you love milk and cream
And my rice puddings are a dream
Perhaps you do have a sweet tooth
Hear's a pudding, let's see the proof.

HADDOCK TREAT

I did have a tasty treat
Haddock was ate not meat
Was so salty, I did think
Like a sponge, I had to drink.

You also had some of mine
Enjoyed it too, seemed fine
Suddenly quick as a wink
You caught drip's in the sink.

BLOATED

Your still cat napping on my bed
After that fish you've been fed
Your so bloated, like a furry ball
You wont be able to move at all
I expect you will sleep all day long
Whilst on my bed, you are in the wrong.

FISHY

Sardines on toast
I love the most
My favourite snack
Behind your back
But aromas from a tin
Do linger from my bin
Once you find me out
Guilty without a doubt.

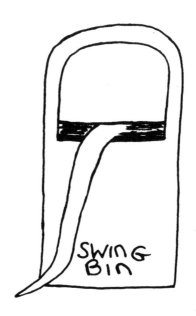

CAT STINT

If ever there was a hint
I witnessed such a stint
For my house is quite old
Very draughty, I've been told.

Your bed was upside down
Which did make me frown
I knew then, how cold you were
When a gust rippled your fur.

BATH TIME

I often sing whilst taking a bath
And it's enough to make a cat laugh
Outside the door you wait patiently
Never impressed it's plain to see.

As bubbly foam survived
In you jumped, well , dived
As the effervescent fizz
Just made you slide and whiz.

WINDOW SEAT

In the window, snoozing in the sun
Chasing flies, thinking it's fun
Passer's by, smile at your antics
Window's, smeared with your lick's.

Now you've found, and play with a bee
You will get stung, that's plain to see
Leave him alone, he does sound mad
You naughty cat, you're ever so bad.

Net curtains flutter in the breeze
Particles of dust, make me sneeze
Making you jump, you lose your balance
Falling off, and hanging from the valance.

cont

Why ornaments aren't knocked flying
Some days, you really are trying
Nothing broken, not yet anyway
I move them around, a few times in a day.

You hide when people call to you
Try to coax with titbits to chew
Wary, hiding under furniture
Give the game away, begin to purr.

Curtains are drawn, late at night
Peep from behind, keeping me in sight
Rustling the newspaper, whilst I read
Leap on my lap,curiosity indeed.

PENS

Every time I want to write
There's never a pen in sight
Pens are mine, not playthings
Need them if the phone rings.

What if I write a letter
Saying, I'm feeling better
Down the side of the armchair
Every one, and their all there.

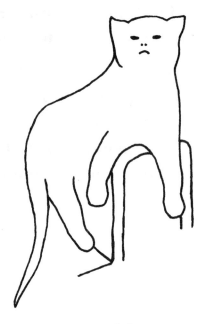

LOTTERY

I always do the lottery
A lucky charm next to me
But I've never ever won
As its only a bit of fun.

A black cat crossed my path
I won ten pounds, what a laugh
If you were only, all black
I might win a million, in one whack.

GLOWING

Glancing out of the window at night
I more than often do get a fright
Many's the time, I come to realise
Those glowing coals are only your eyes.

FRIGHT

You gave me such a fright
In the middle of the night
Whilst I lay in a sleep
Which was ever so deep
It was really quite absurd
How I was noisily disturbed
As you chased around the house
After a poor little mouse.

STRANGLED

What a shock I usually get
Whilst nodding off, you artful pet
I try to relax, as darkness falls
As around my neck, you wind your paws.

You never like me to doze
Or read a book I suppose
Perhaps you feel neglected
Seems different when I'm in bed.

HOT WATER BOTTLE

My hot water bottle, has a grey furry case
On my feet every night, in the same place
The cover, my friend said, was once a hat
What! I stammered. did you say a CAT!

It might be fluffy and grey
But my friend said on that day
She bought it from a jumble sale
But sneezed when she did inhale.

RESIDENT PIP

As in a home, I called to see
A dear lady in time for tea
Pip. A beautiful fluffy cat
Strolled over to where I sat.

Pip just loved my velvet skirt
Was on my lap , quite alert
So fidgety, causing a stir
Now my skirts covered in fur.

RESIDENT CLOWY

Clowy the resident cat
Found it awkward when sat
For he had fallen off a wall
Broke his leg, toes and all.

So his leg was in a plaster
Now he cant move any faster
Walking now isn't much fun
Lift one, swing one, drop one.

MY FRIEND'S PING PONG

Ping Pong was a Siamese
Had a cough and a wheeze
Her mistress was anxious
Took her to a vet, on a bus
The vet said what is wrong
Oh it's my poor Ping Pong
The woman cried quite upset
She will be fine. Said the vet
Peering in Ping Pongs ears
You really have no fears
Her ears are blue, so cold
She's deaf as the ears have a fold.

NECKLACE

Necklace broke, beads were everywhere
Lost for choice, you just had to stare
Coloured beads, were chased all around
Hitting the skirting, with an awful sound.

The necklace was a present
Come through the post from Kent
The beads are lost that's for sure
Rolled down the cracks in the floor.

GOLD FISH

Swimming around and around
Was a fish who made no sound
Until you stirred with a paw
Causing the fish bowl to fall.

Although the bowl didn't break
I said, for goodness sake
You're in disgrace, that's for sure
You've had your fish. There's no more.

POSY

My lounge is quite cosy
The garden's nice and rosy
A neighbours cat called Posy
Stare's through my window. Nosy.

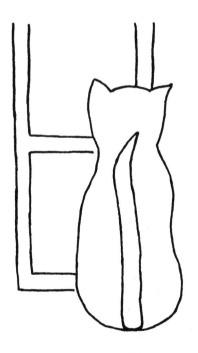

41

BATTLE

The fur's been flying, I can tell
Goodness me, you don't look well
I heard a noise, late last night
And really think you've been in a fight
Like a Banshee, I heard you wail
There's such a bend and kink in your tail
I think you're in dire need of a nap
Just don't hope, to take it on my lap.

RAT

I have a big cat
Who sits on a mat
He gets a pat
Looks a bit fat
Like a furry hat
Once chased a rat
Put it where I sat.

BOXING CLEVER

There were holes in a box lid
Quite safe as you often hid
But when the vicar came to tea
This large box sidled up to me.

The vicar said well I never
Something's boxing clever
For you rolled over on top
Walking in the holes, non-stop.

JOYFUL

A little baby was bought to me
A visitor I was so glad to see
She was then placed on my knee
The baby gurgled so joyfully
Instantly you were in the pram
Attacking the rattles. Wham.

CAT SHOW

Showing them off, how can they choose
All are appealing, no matter whose
Glossy coats, are all spruced up
I wonder who will win a silver cup.

The judge has stopped at a tortoiseshell
An owner fuss's, to be sure all is well
So many different cats to be seen
One is spitting, and looks rather mean.

Nearly finished, almost coming to a close
All the showing, takes a while, I suppose
At long last, the winner for this year
Gosh. A ginger tom ? Oh, my dear!

GINGER TOM

A cat the colour of marmalade
Saw our tree, and sat in the shade
Then a squirrel just had to run
Dropping it's nut's, one by one.

FEAR

A huge great spider, did venture near
I have a phobia, and always a fear
Too close for comfort, heading for me
Long hairy legs, with a black body.

Where are you cat, you can't be out
Soon I'll be screaming, and I'll shout
Are you hiding, or just fallen asleep
I'm too much a coward, to come and peep.

GRAZED

You've had many a graze
In quite a number of ways
But being as your a cat
With nine lives, and all that
Hopefully you will prove it wrong
And live on and on, ever so long.

CRAFTY

I cannot see you but heard your meow
I've hunted high and low, and worried so
Searched in the cupboards, under the bed
Surely I'll see you when its time to be fed.

Up and down the stairs, out of the house
Where else to search, it's quiet as a mouse
Ever so loudly, I call your name
Go on ignore me, It's always the same.

Cont

So curious you have always been
Usually exploring, not always seen
It's in your nature, I understand
Good job I haven't got lots of land.

I'll try to be crafty, rattle your dish
Make you believe you are having fish
It really worked, your back at last
Came running to meet me, ever so fast.

A DOG

Next door's dog, is enormous
And he's terribly boisterous
But chasing you was a howler
Just missing you by a whisker.

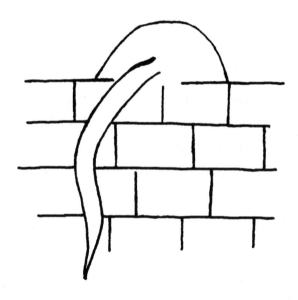

HAT

Haven't seen that before
Its new and on the floor
Looks quite familiar
seems to make you purr
Fluffy and bright red
Now its in your bed
No, its not another cat
Just a pom pom from my hat.

CRADLE

A cats cradle, is there such a thing
Wherever you are, you always swing
Inside the house, or in the street
Any position, you land on your feet.

ON THE TILES

In the bathroom hanging
I left a necklace swaying
Unfortunately for me
You noticed immediately.

It sounded like tap dancing
Curiosity had me advancing
Watching you jig on the tiles
Embedded beads. Hidden smiles.

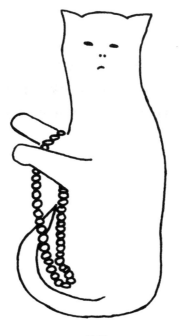

TROLLEY TRAIN

I have a shopping trolley
Which you use more, by golly
Propped up inside a cupboard
With rubbish, what a hoard.

It's your adventure site
More so than ever at night
You wheel it out like a train
Then around the room again.

CHURNED

Whenever I spin all my washing
You sit on top, as it's sloshing
And the milk you've just sipped
Will surely turn to cream. Whipped.

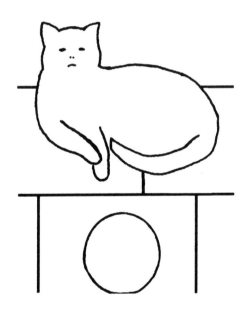

NINE LIVES

A Persian cat or a Siamese
A ginger tom, if you please
Little kitten's, soft as velvet
So much adored, as a loving pet.

Some are fluffy, with long fur
Stroke them, and they really purr
Indeed of course, some are so white
And really do, stand out at night.

But a witches cat, is midnight black
Supposed good luck, across ones track
Snazzy stripe's are also attractive
And all cats have nine lives to live.

VACUUM CLEANER

When I do the housework, once a week
It's like a game, called hide and seek
You hide away, so still, so concealed
Then leap out when the vacuum's wheeled.

Black Cat

The dream I had last night
Gave me such a fright
For on a broomstick sat
Were you ,a witches cat.

You both sailed so high
In the black velvet sky
As dropped stars shimmered
A full moon glimmered.

Cont

Her cackling laugh arose
I saw her long crooked nose
For my dream was so clear
I called, you couldn't hear.

Her long hair was flowing
Your green eyes glowing
As on and on you flew
Then the alarm went. Phew.

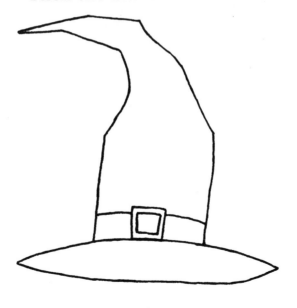

OUT OF THE BAG

I bought a birthday surprise
For a young man with no ties
Thought I'd lost the price tag
You let the cat out of the bag.

AUTUMN

When late autumn's in the air
The tree's do appear to be bare
Raking leaves, just make me shout
As gale force winds blow them about.

But to you dear cat, it's amusing
Chasing each leaf, so entertaining
As my pile just seems to flutter
Watching you, I stare and mutter.

Oh no, I thought you would do that
You are a ninny, you silly cat
For the holly leaves, are brittle
And you've just found a prickle.

WEATHER

The wind did blow, the sky was grey
Some of my washing, almost blew away
But my smalls still fluttered like flags
Thanks to you cat, now covered in snags.

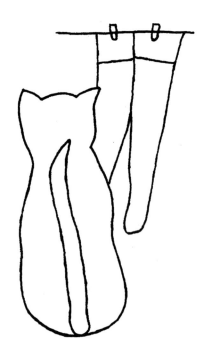

VEXED

I almost know where
The Fox has its lair
near the compost heap
Where you go to sleep.

I saw it this morning
So early I was yawning
You did kind of bristle
As I tried to whistle.

It was thirsty, parched
You wailed, back arched
Spitting you chased it away
But it wanted to play.

BUTTERFLIES

Beautiful, colourful, butterflies
Always attract your impish eye's
Delicate fluttering, look so playful
Gazing at them will never be dull.

HALLOWEEN

Trick or treat its Halloween
But you are nowhere to be seen
Their masks are scary, I do realise
They're only children who fantasise.

I might have some biscuits, no sweets
I wasn't prepared for such treats
I've my favourite treacle tart, yum
Here you are children, do have some.

Oh there you are, you silly cat
Here are the children with a bat
So realistic, I am admitting
Stop it cat, stop that spitting.

HEDGEHOG

Vegetable peelings, on the compost heap
As it's so warm, I find hedgehogs asleep
Usually you lurk, and creep all around
Listening for scratching, or any sound.

STALKING

Stalking through the grass so high
Something of interest, you did spy
An insect or a wee mouse, probably
I'll get that grass cut, You'll see.

I hope you haven't caught butterflies
It wouldn't be much of a surprise
Anything that is airborne
You're so mesmerised and forlorn.

GHOSTIES

Vampires and bats, so spine chilling
Was a film on the telly, I was viewing
It was reassuring having you next to me
Meow. Yes come and sit on my knee.

Its been on for, almost an hour
And I was shrinking with horror
Its such a comfort, your so near
Purring on my lap. I've no fear.

cont

Don't you extend your sharp claws
You must be careful with those paws
Now your off by the fire I suppose
After ripping my brand new hose.

Ghostly shadows followed me to bed
The wind was moaning I read instead.
Branches clawed the window .Is it a bat
It's you behind the curtains scaredy cat.

BIRD TABLE

When I put out food, on the bird table
Don't you climb, as I know your able
I usually feed them, always encourage
So don't slink out from under a hedge.

As they flutter, whilst having a bath
It's so amusing, it makes me laugh
But you tiptoe, utterly mesmerised
Once more, yet again, you're chastised.

GNOME

In the garden there's a gnome
Nearby where you always roam
A fishing rod he does hold
Standing there, big and bold.

You nearly always saunter by
Giving him a mischievous eye
Your tail forever twitching
The line continuously swishing.

CLIMBER

What are you doing up that tree
You're after all those magpies
Come right down here instantly
Leave them alone or otherwise
There seems to be more than two
And they will surely go for you
Your tail will have a tweak
As they clamp it in their beak
You will then topple over and fall
As the tree is an oak and so tall.

TELEVISION

When I watch the telly, I'm confused
As you always seem to be so amused
Adverts definitely have your esteem
As you peer at lush adverts and dream.

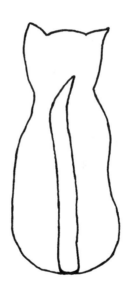

ADVERTISING

Always popular the cat has been
Rain or shine its always seen
Usually found asleep by day
Alert at night ready to play.

The cat is used in advertising
Especially milk, there's a thing
Cat food of coarse, top of the list
And a coal fire, a cat would insist.

Also a cat takes part in cartoons
Usually a hero, with nice tunes
Or chasing a mouse or a bird
Like Tom and Sylvester. Absurd.

SCARF

My lovely scarf, my blue chiffon
Was my favourite, always had it on
But in a draft, it fluttered to the floor
I haven't got my lovely scarf anymore.

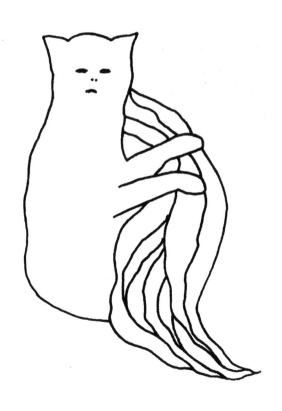

NETS

My curtains are in tatters
You find it never matters
And honestly, to be frank
There's no money in the bank.

My nets were lovely, when new
That was long before I had you
But looking in from the outside
The shame I feel, I want to hide.

Cont

I know you love the window sill
And climb the nets, you always will
So what if we come to a compromise
Like heavily starched. Penny wise.

I don't think I could be without you
Oh, he's doing it again, Shoo
I might as well just give in
What ever I do, Ill never win.

FROG

As I went to get a large log
Low and behold, I saw a frog
It sat so still, so Immobile
You sniffed it so natural.

GARDENING

I've planted lettuce and beetroot
Keeping an eye, for cats in pursuit
Being they all walk through and stay
In my garden, any time of the day.

Must be seven, could well be more
They spy the birds, from the floor
And when I dig the vegetable patch
Worms tempt the birds, they watch.

PUSS IN BOOTS

In my gardening boots are kept
Usually you, as you've slept
You've never given two hoots
Just looking like puss in boots.

MOUSE

You placed a mouse at my feet
I scrambled on the nearest seat
Look what I bought, you seemed to say
Not a very good start to the day
Take it away, get rid of it
While I compose myself and sit.

CRAFTY

I cannot see you but heard your meow
Really hunted high and low
Searched in the cupboards, under the bed
Surely I'll see you when its time to be fed.

Up and down the stairs, out of the house
Where else to search, it's quiet as a mouse
Ever so loudly, I call your name
You ignore me, It's always the same.

Cont

So curious you have always been
Usually exploring, not always seen
It's in your nature, I understand
Good job I haven't got lots of land.

I'll try to be crafty, rattle your dish
Make you believe you are having fish
It really worked, your back at last
Came running to meet me, ever so fast.

SNOWFLAKES

Snowflakes sprinkled the window sill
Curious fascination, kept you still
As feathery flakes silently fell
You were mute, as your tinkling bell.

The sun did try to send it's rays
You like a glow on such cold days
At long last you landed on the mat
By the log fire, which just spat.

SNOWBOUND

Plodding through the deep deep snow
Now which way are you going to go
As you seem to be heading for home
Down through the garden, so alone.

It's going to be a bit of a struggle
And I hate snow, that's the trouble
But you're doing fine, keep going on
Now he's disappeared. Where's he gone.

MERRY XMAS

On my Xmas holiday
You also came to stay
So welcome we were made
My room was where you laid.

My friend also loves cats
And has two, Mits and Mats
Being Manx, they have no tails
They nip yours, amidst wails.

THAWED

Everywhere is crisp and white
with not a single soul in sight
A few footprints, here and there
But not mine, I wouldn't dare.

You wander for a slinky stroll
Then you slide and begin to roll
Hurtling, you bump the back door
Where melted snow fell to the floor.

From the roof slid such a heap
You were stuck, and couldn't leap
Opening the door, what a surprise
A snowman, with real paws and eyes.

CHRISTMAS TREE

Christmas is here, and we've got our tree
Colourful decoration's will hang festively
First I'll spray well, the imitation snow
Oop's, Oh dear, I'm sorry cat, DON'T GO.

At last the tree is beautifully dressed
With trimming that glitter at it's best
Seeing your reflection in a glass ball
You purred in awe, as the tree did fall.

Misty

Gently padding over the bed
A cat woke her Mistress up instead
Hello Misty a sleepy voice did say
I've missed you, while you've been away.

Usually some evenings you sit nearby
Such tender moments, it makes me sigh
I love to see you, and have no fears
Even though, you've been dead for years.

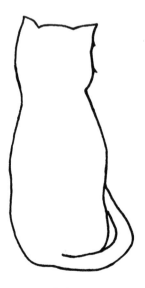